Paint My Room!

Written by Roger Carr
Illustrated by Peter Paul Bajer

sundance™

"Time to get up!" Mom said.

"Put on your old clothes," Dad said. "We're going to paint your room today."

Nick sat up.

It was the weekend. Mom and Dad always did something exciting on the weekend.

3

"What color will we paint it?"
Nick asked.

"You choose," Dad said. "It's your room."

Nick looked all around the room.
Then he had a great idea.

"Let's paint it like a jungle!"

"Painting a jungle will take a long time," said Mom.

"Can we paint the trees first?" Nick asked.

"OK," Mom said.
"Let's get the cans of paint."

Dad put down a big sheet.

They put the cans of paint on the sheet and they all started painting trees.

That night, Nick slept in his jungle room under the jungle trees.

"I like sleeping in the jungle," he said.

The next day they painted monkeys and birds. Dad and Nick were good at painting monkeys.
Mom was very good at painting birds.

Nick painted a lion and a tiger.

Then they all painted more lions and tigers.

"Now I will paint an elephant,"
Nick said.

"Can I paint a giant snake?"
asked Dad.

11

That night, when Nick went to bed, he could not sleep.

The lions looked very fierce.
The tigers looked very hungry.

Nick got up and turned on the light.

13

The next morning, when Nick woke up,
he lay in bed and looked at the animals

Then he had an idea.
He found the cans of paint
and the brushes.

He painted a smile on the lion's face.
He painted a smile on the tiger's face.
He painted a smile on the snake's face,
and he painted smiles on the birds.

"That's better," he said.

That night, when he went to bed,
Nick smiled at his animal friends.
"Good night," he said

and turned off the light.